Bibliographic information published by the German National Library:

The German National Library lists this publication in the National Bibliography; detailed bibliographic data are available on the Internet at http://dnb.dnb.de .

Imprint:

Copyright © 2017 GRIN Verlag, Open Publishing GmbH
Print and binding: Books on Demand GmbH, Norderstedt Germany
ISBN: 9783668537330

This book at GRIN:

http://www.grin.com/en/e-book/376403/artificial-intelligence-and-blockchains-in-financial-services-potential

Aditi Shet Shirodkar

Artificial Intelligence and Blockchains in financial services. Potential applications, challenges, and risks

GRIN Publishing

GRIN - Your knowledge has value

Since its foundation in 1998, GRIN has specialized in publishing academic texts by students, college teachers and other academics as e-book and printed book. The website www.grin.com is an ideal platform for presenting term papers, final papers, scientific essays, dissertations and specialist books.

Visit us on the internet:

http://www.grin.com/

http://www.facebook.com/grincom

http://www.twitter.com/grin_com

ARTIFICIAL INTELLIGENCE AND BLOCKCHAINS: HOW ARE THESE TECHNOLOGIES CURRENTLY APPLIED IN FINANCIAL SERVICES? WHAT ARE THE POTENTIAL FUTURE APPLICATIONS AND THE CHALLENGES OR RISKS INVOLVED?

Aditi Shet Shirodkar

ABSTRACT

Artificial Intelligence (AI) and Blockchain technologies have been at the centre of research in the for the past couple of years. AI is more widely used and implemented by Tech companies and we come across it in some form or another in our daily lives. Bitcoin (the original Blockchain) is also gaining popularity. Financial Industry however have been slow in accepting these technologies due to several reasons such as need for higher security in financial firms, some shortfalls in the technologies, lack of standardized regulations etc. There are certain firms who have taken up the initiative to work in these fields and have come up with various Proof-Of-Concepts (POCs) specifically for the financial industry. These are in the form of private projects or open source ones like Hyperledger hosted by Linux. There also firms that are working towards integrating the two. These technologies are individually effective, but integrating the two could provide better and faster solutions. Both these technologies, AI and Blockchain, will prove to be disruptive. AI would make our lives easier and more efficient while Blockchain would provide us with a secure and decentralized data system. Effective use of both these technologies would provide considerable cost benefits to financial institutions.

KEYWORDS

Artificial Intelligence

Big Data

Machine Learning

Blockchains

Distributed Ledger Technology

Financial Services

Financial Industry

ABBREVIATIONS USED

AI   Artificial Intelligence

ML   Machine Learning

DLT   Distributed Ledger Technology

FTC   Federal Trade Commission

AWS   Amazon Web Services

AML   Anti-Money Laundering

KYC   Know-Your-Customer

CDD   Customer Due Diligence

RTGS   Real Time Gross Settlement

NASDAQ   National Association of Securities Dealers Automated Quotations

DTCC   Depository Trust and Clearing Corporation

IoT   Internet of Things

POC   Proof of Concept

P2P   Peer to Peer

CTO   Chief Technology Officer

IP   Intellectual Property

DAO   Decentralized Autonomous Organizations

DoS   Denial of Service

SWIFT   Society for Worldwide Interbank Financial Telecommunication

LIST OF FIGURES

TABLE OF CONTENTS

CHAPTER 1 – INTRODUCTION

1.1 Research Background

According to a survey conducted by Synechron Inc., Financial executives believe Artificial Intelligence (AI) and Blockchains will revolutionise the Financial Industry[1]. AI or Machine Learning (ML) is a technology used to collect and analyse massive amounts of data (Big Data) to identify patterns and to do predictive modelling. These predictions could then be used to provide personalized services to clients and used in making strategic decisions for a firm to improve efficiency and productivity. Blockchain, also known as Distributed Ledger Technology (DLT), involves an immutable distributed digital ledger of transactions. The immutable nature of the ledger makes it highly secure. Federal Trade Commission (FTC) organized FinTech Forum event in March 2017, where a group of distinguished panellists discussed the impacts of these two technologies[2].

As a part of Science Fiction, AI has been a part of our lives for quite some time, while Blockchain is a relatively unknown concept. Even though AI technology has not developed humanoid robot capability, the Tech companies like Amazon have been using and have recently started providing Big Data solutions such as Amazon Web Services (AWS)[3]. The research in Blockchain on the other hand is in its nascent stages. However, the use of both these technologies in Financial Services is not widespread and needs further research.

---

[1] Finance Execs Believe AI and Blockchain Will Revolutionise Industry. (2016, June 08). Retrieved May 28, 2017, from http://www.fintech.finance/01-news/finance-execs-believe-ai-and-blockchain-will-revolutionise-industry/

[2] FinTech Forum: Artificial Intelligence and Blockchain. (2017, March 09). Retrieved May 28, 2017, from https://www.ftc.gov/news-events/events-calendar/2017/03/fintech-forum-blockchain-artificial-intelligence

[3] Big Data Use Cases – Amazon Web Services (AWS). (n.d.). Retrieved May 28, 2017, from https://aws.amazon.com/big-data/use-cases/

1.2 Aim and Objectives of the Dissertation

The aim of this dissertation is to identify the use cases for AI and Blockchain technologies in the Financial Services. It will also provide the possible applications for these technologies in the future and identify the challenges and risks of using the same. The objectives of the dissertation are:

a) Examine the literature that discusses use cases of AI and Blockchain in Financial Services.

b) Examine the literature that discusses the possibilities of integrating the two technologies[4].

c) Examine the literature that discusses the challenges of using these technologies.

d) Identify the current use cases of AI and Blockchains in Financial Services

e) Identify the future of AI and Blockchains in Financial Services

f) Identify the risks of using AI and Blockchains in Financial Services

1.3 Research Questions

a) Why are AI and Blockchain still not as used widely used in Financial Services as they are in Tech companies (especially AI, Blockchain is new to both)?

b) What are the challenges for implementation of these technologies into the Financial Sector?

c) What are the possible advantages of integrating the two technologies?

d) What are the possible future applications of these technologies in the Financial Sector and what would be the risks involved in doing the same?

---

[4] State Street Wants to Monetize Blockchain With Artificial Intelligence. (2017, May 17). Retrieved May 28, 2017, from http://www.coindesk.com/street-street-is-betting-ai-can-help-monetize-blockchain-tech/

1.4 Structure of the Dissertation

The aim of this first chapter is to provide an overview of the subjects that will be discussed through the course of this dissertation. It is important to identify the aim and objectives, as they provide the guidelines that will help establish a framework for the research. This is an analytical study of AI and Blockchain Technologies as applied in Financial Services.

The dissertation is further divided into four chapters:

a) Literature Review – this chapter will evaluate existing literature on the subject and report important findings. This will help the reader to better understand the concepts and the applications of the technologies in the industry in general.

b) Research Methodologies – this chapter will describe the methodologies used to collect, examine and analyse the research data. It will also help to establish if the data collected covers all aspects of the situation.

c) Discussion and Analysis – this chapter will answer the research questions posed above. The focus will be on the challenges and the future of the technologies in the industry.

d) Conclusion – this chapter will be used to summarize the key findings, provide personal insights and observations on the topic discussed. It will also discuss limitations of the research.

CHAPTER 2 – LITERATURE REVIEW

2.1 Introduction

The purpose of this chapter is to evaluate the literature related to applications of Artificial

Intelligence and Blockchain technologies in the Financial Industry to give the researcher an

understanding of the two technologies and their applications. The first section will provide an

overview of AI and Blockchain technologies and their distinct features. The next two sections

will discuss why the Financial Institutions are investing in AI and Blockchain, followed by a

few examples of the existing use cases (of AI and Blockchain) in the industry. This will

demonstrate what has already been done, before determining out what can be done further.

Lastly, an analysis is presented of the challenges and risks involved in the implementation of

these technologies as well as the research which focuses on integrating the two for better

outcomes.

2.2 Overview of AI and Blockchain technologies

Artificial Intelligence is the technology which enables a machine to think and act like a

human. Even though we are far from successfully achieving the Turing Test[5], machines

which are indistinguishable from humans, in recent years there has been a lot of progress in

building smarter machines. Some of the capabilities AI can provide are:

1) Ability to analyse Big Data – considering the tremendous volume of data generated

   through Big Data, AI is necessary for analysis.

---

[5] What is Turing test? - Definition from WhatIs.com. (n.d.). Retrieved June 17, 2017, from
http://whatis.techtarget.com/definition/Turing-Test

2) Ability to analyse unstructured data – data obtained from Big Data sources may not always be structured, that is in a regular or tabular form. Unstructured data is difficult for humans to analyse. AI can be used to identify patterns in unstructured data and provide insights that can help solve real world problems by predictive modelling such as product customization, market segmentation etc.

3) Machine Learning – AI has the capability to train a machine, like humans. Machines are provided with large sets of real world data and an initial set of instructions. The machine is then left to learn and adapt according to the data. Neural networks are used to train a machine to analyse like a human brain.

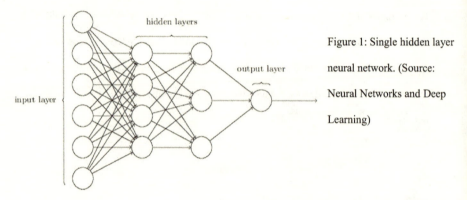

Figure 1: Single hidden layer neural network. (Source: Neural Networks and Deep Learning)

4) Visual Analysis – the machine learning capabilities can be utilised for visual analysis such as Facial Recognition (e.g. Facebook picture tags), Pattern Recognition etc. One example is the Clinical Decision Support systems used in the healthcare industry to analyse medical reports and recommend treatments to patients, by comparing patient's medical history with the data from existing medical databases.

5) Sound Analysis – AI can also be used for sound analysis. AI can be trained to identify its user's voice and provide personalized responses (e.g. - Apple's Siri).

6) Natural Language Capabilities (NLC) – AI can learn to talk or respond like humans. In this case an AI assistant can be trained to respond in natural language (such as plain English). If trained correctly it should be impossible for a human to distinguish that it is talking to a machine.

Blockchain or Distributed Ledger Technology is a decentralized database which stores data, in the form of immutable blocks which are validated using a peer-to-peer (P2P) consensus mechanism. It is combination of multiple technologies and is highly secure. The salient features of Blockchain technology are:

1) Decentralized authority – blocks are added to the blockchain using a P2P consensus mechanism. There is no single controlling body which authorizes the transactions. This is a huge change from how the current financial institutions function, where a trusted organization (like a bank) has control of transactions.

2) Distributed database – the data added in blockchain is stored on every single node which is part of the chain. Hence if one of the nodes get corrupted or attacked there is always a copy available on all the other nodes to fall back on. This makes the blockchain less susceptible to data loss or corruption.

3) Consensus Mechanism – a block is added to the blockchain once it is accepted by majority of the nodes in the blockchain. Every node in the chain has equal power, and a node is free to quit or join the chain at will. The only way the system can be overpowered is if an attacker has enough computing power to run more than 51% of the nodes, i.e. 51 % attack[6].

4) Tamper-proof (immutable) data – once a block is formed by a node it takes a certain amount of time to get validated by nodes. Once a block is successfully validated it gets added to the blockchain. After a certain number of blocks get added after a block, the data added to the block becomes immutable. One cannot modify an older block without modifying all other blocks formed since then till the latest block. This makes the information added to a blockchain tamper resistant.

---

[6] Floyd, D. (2017, June 06). 51% Attack. Retrieved June 17, 2017, from
http://www.investopedia.com/terms/1/51-attack.asp

5) Transparency of data – data added to a blockchain is completely transparent as the ledger is public to all nodes which are part of the blockchain. This feature provides a means for everyone to validate the data and build trust. As the data is visible to all and tamper proof once it is added to a blockchain it is public knowledge.

2.3 Why are Financial Institutions investing in AI?

Research in AI has been going for much longer than the research in Blockchain. The technology has had times where there has been surges in research funding followed by periods called "AI winters" where the research was stagnant. In the past couple of years there has been high activity of mergers and acquisitions with AI firms (refer Figure 2).

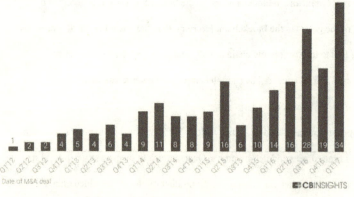

Figure 2: Artificial Intelligence Mergers and Acquisition Activity (Source: CB Insights)

When research in AI halts, it cases an AI winter, but when something new is discovered a surge is provided to research activities. Recent developments in technology have resulted in more activity in the field than ever before, as can be seen from above figure. The reasons for this are:

1) Emergence of Big Data – due to social media and other sources there is tremendous amount of data generated every minute[7]. The 7 V's of Big Data are Volume, Velocity, Variety, Variability, Veracity, Visualization and Value[8]. Most of this data is unstructured. A human can't analyse this data, it requires massive computational abilities and hence requires AI.

2) Convenience of data storage – not only has the amount of data increased, the availability of platforms such as "the cloud" has made storing this data much more convenient. Tech companies like Google offer secure cloud data storage services for affordable prices[9] and this has changed the way firms store and access their data.

3) Increase in Computational Power – Moore's Law states that computational power approximately doubles every year[10]. This observation was made in 1965 and has been true ever since. Computer processers are getting faster every day and we are finding new means to utilise this power.

4) Development of better algorithms – recent development in Neural Network and Deep Learning[11] is exactly the kind of breakthrough that was needed to build AI. This technology allows a machine to form a net of neurons like a human brain. This system is then provided with data and trained to learn as humans do. This branch of science is called deep learning and is the one used to make an AI machine.

---

[7] How Big Data Is Empowering AI and Machine Learning at Scale. (2017, May 08). Retrieved June 18, 2017, from http://sloanreview.mit.edu/article/how-big-data-is-empowering-ai-and-machine-learning-at-scale/

[8] The 7 V's of Big Data. (2016, August 18). Retrieved June 18, 2017, from https://www.impactradius.com/blog/7-vs-big-data/

[9] Cloud Storage - Online Data Storage | Google Cloud Platform. (n.d.). Retrieved June 18, 2017, from https://cloud.google.com/storage/

[10] Staff, I. (2003, November 24). Moore's Law. Retrieved June 18, 2017, from http://www.investopedia.com/terms/m/mooreslaw.asp

[11] Nielsen, M. A. (n.d.). Neural Networks and Deep Learning. Retrieved June 18, 2017, from http://neuralnetworksanddeeplearning.com/

All the above factors create the perfect environment for firms to start investing in AI. The aim of AI is to build a system that would perform a task as effectively as or, in most cases, better than a trained human would. Also, a machine would be devoid of human limitations. It would not tire out, and would work with the same level of efficiency – 24/7. If designed well, a machine could perform a task much faster and with fewer errors. Investing in AI has always been advantageous, it was only a matter of time until the technology was advanced enough to build it.

2.4 Why are Financial Institutions investing in Blockchains?

Compared to AI, Blockchain technology is nascent. It was first introduced in 2008 by Satoshi Nakamoto[12]. Blockchain is the next revolution in technology which has the potential to disrupt financial industry and completely restructure the way it currently functions.

BLOCKCHAIN QUARTERLY GLOBAL FINANCING HISTORY
Q1'12 - Q1'17

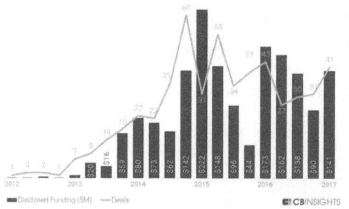

Figure 3: Blockchain Quarterly Global Financing History (Source: CB Insights)

---

[12] Nakamoto, S. (2008). Bitcoin: A Peer-to-Peer Electronic Cash System. 1-9. Retrieved June 18, 2017, from https://bitcoin.org/bitcoin.pdf.

If blockchain solutions are successfully implemented they could result in huge cost benefits

for financial institutions. This is the reason why there has been a surge in funding for

Blockchain research recently (refer Figure 3). A few areas in which Blockchain could provide

benefits with an economy of scale are discussed below:

1) Money Laundering – Global money laundering transactions are estimated at roughly

   U.S. $1-2 trillion annually[13]. Financial Institutions also spend considerable amount of

   time and money on Anti-Money Laundering (AML) efforts. If not, they would end up

   paying fines to regulators for non-compliance of AML regulations. A decentralized

   and immutable database would therefore be useful to tackle these issues.

2) Tighter Know-Your-Customer (KYC) and Customer Due Diligence (CDD) Norms – A

   global survey conducted by Thomson Reuters indicated that the costs and complexity

   of KYC are rising. While a financial firm's average costs to meet the obligations are

   $60 million, some of them are spending up to $500 million on compliance with KYC

   and CDD norms[14]. A distributed KYC registry on Blockchain technology would

   reduce duplication of client information and keep it secure.

3) Latency in Trade Settlements – in financial trading the settlement process usually takes

   a few days[15]. Reducing the settlement time and removing intermediaries would result

   in providing cost benefits to the firms. Blockchain solutions would help eliminate

   intermediaries and reduce settlement time to minutes.

---

[13] P. (n.d.). Anti-Money Laundering. Retrieved June 19, 2017, from
http://www.pwc.com/gx/en/services/advisory/forensics/economic-crime-survey/anti-money-laundering.html

[14] Thomson Reuters 2016 Know Your Customer Surveys Reveal Escalating Costs and
Complexity. (2016, May 09). Retrieved June 19, 2017, from
https://www.thomsonreuters.com/en/press-releases/2016/may/thomson-reuters-2016-know-your-customer-surveys.html

[15] Understanding the SETTLEMENT PROCESS. (n.d.). Retrieved June 19, 2017, from
http://www.dtcc.com/understanding-settlement/index.html

4) Regulatory challenges – financial institutions face various regulatory challenges such as multiple sources of data, multiple and dynamic report formats, lack of skilled resources, inaccuracy of data, stringency of timelines, etc. Globally, approximately $80 billion is spent on governance, risk and compliance, and the market is only expected to grow, reaching $120 billion in the next five years. Financial institutions in the US alone have paid more than $160 billion in fines for non-compliance[16].

2.5 Existing Use Cases of AI in Financial Industry

AI has applications across all industries. It is the disruptive technology which aims to make our jobs faster and easier. AI is being widely used by Tech Firms and the benefits it has provided to them has lead Financial Institutions to invest in the technology. A few firms in financial sector which have realized the potential of AI and capitalized on it are:

1) UBS (Union Bank of Switzerland) – the largest Swiss Bank has been at the forefront for AI utilization in the financial sector. In 2014, UBS teamed up with the Tech company Sqreem to provide personalized services to its wealthy clients using AI[17]. Since then the bank has utilised AI in various other fields in the organization in collaboration with Istituto Dalle Molle di Studi sull'Intelligenza Artificiale (IDSIA) – the Swiss AI Lab – as published in its white paper[18]

---

[16]Regulatory Reporting: Don't Play Catchup! (2017, March 15). Retrieved June 19, 2017, from https://letstalkpayments.com/regulatory-reporting-dont-play-catchup/

[17] UBS uses artificial intelligence to deliver personalised advice to wealthy clients. (2014, December 09). Retrieved June 20, 2017, from http://www.scmp.com/business/banking-finance/article/1659205/ubs-uses-artificial-intelligence-deliver-personalised

[18] UBS. (2017). Intelligent Automation. 1-25. Retrieved June 20, 2017, from https://www.ubs.com/magazines/innovation/en/into-the-future/2017/ai-and-financial-services.html

2) Goldman Sachs Groups – the American multinational finance company is also among the first ones to invest in AI. In 2014, Goldman Sachs invested $15 Million in AI Tech company Kensho[19]. Kensho's cloud based software can find answers to millions of financial question combinations in an instant by scanning nearly every financial asset on the planet. The system also has natural language capabilities which means it can provide answers in plain English. Kensho's "AI for Investors" is valued at over $500 million in funding round from Wall Street[20].

3) BBVA (Banco Bilbao Vizcaya Argentaria) – the multinational Spanish bank along with a Tech Start-up Das-Nano has formed the biometrics technology company Veridas[21]. The aim of this firm is to develop client authentication and authorization system using AI.

4) Genworth Financial – the Fortune 500 insurance company designed an end-to-end system based on AI to automate the underwriting of Long Term Care (LTC) and Life Insurance applications[22]. A "fuzzy logic rule engine" encodes the underwriter's guidelines and an evolutionary algorithm optimizes the engine's performance. Finally, a natural language parser is used to improve the coverage of the underwriting system.

[19] Broun A. (2014, November 24). Goldman Sachs Leads $15 Million Investment in Kensho. Retrieved June 20, 2017, from http://www.prnewswire.com/news-releases/goldman-sachs-leads-15-million-investment-in-kensho-300000102.html

[20] Gara, A. (2017, February 28). Kensho's AI For Investors Just Got Valued At Over $500 Million In Funding Round From Wall Street. Retrieved June 20, 2017, from https://www.forbes.com/sites/antoinegara/2017/02/28/kensho-sp-500-million-valuation-jpmorgan-morgan-stanley/#144a4d385cbf

[21] Team, E. (2017, June 20). BBVA spawns new biometrics company Veridas out of two-year startup partnership. Retrieved June 20, 2017, from https://www.finextra.com/newsarticle/30712/bbva-spawns-new-biometrics-company-veridas-out-of-two-year-startup-partnership

[22] Aggour, K., & Cheetham, W. (n.d.). Automating the Underwriting of Insurance Applications. General Electric Global Research, 1-8. Retrieved July 20, 2017, from https://www.aaai.org/Papers/IAAI/2005/IAAI05-001.pdf

5) Binatix – is a deep learning trading start-up firm. It uses machine learning algorithms to spot patterns that offer edge in investing[23]. Unlike most deep learning approaches, Binatix incorporates temporal signals which provide a 3D view of the financial trends minute-by-minute. Some other trading firms which use similar technology are Two Sigma Investments, Cerebellum Capital, KFL Capital, Clone Algo etc[24].

6) AlphaSense – is a firm which runs a smart financial search engine that slashes research time[25]. It gathers relevant public and licensed financial data such as broker research, SEC filings, press releases and tries to understand and interpret the financial language. AlphaSense works with many leading banks such as Credit Suisse, JP Morgan etc. The firm raised $33 million in funding last year[26].

7) Dataminr – is an AI based firm that provides a platform to provide early indication of high-level events by scanning social media platforms[27]. It is used by financial professionals on the buy-side and sell-side to learn about market-moving events earlier and discover differentiating content that can be transformed into sharper insights, better opportunities and more profitable decisions.

---

[23] Temple, J. (2014, September 10). Introducing Binatix: A Deep Learning Trading Firm That's Already Profitable. Retrieved June 20, 2017, from
https://www.recode.net/2014/9/10/11630724/introducing-binatix-a-deep-learning-trading-firm-thats-already

[24] List of Funds or Trading Firms Using Artificial Intelligence or Machine Learning. (2015, May 29). Retrieved June 20, 2017, from https://robusttechhouse.com/list-of-funds-or-trading-firms-using-artificial-intelligence-or-machine-learning/

[25] Intelligent Search. Find What Matters. Fast. (n.d.). Retrieved June 20, 2017, from https://www.alpha-sense.com/

[26] Shin, L. (2016, March 06). AlphaSense, Search Engine For Financial Professionals, Raises $33 Million. Retrieved June 20, 2017, from
https://www.forbes.com/sites/laurashin/2016/03/06/alphasense-search-engine-for-financial-professionals-raises-33-million/#66fdf77960aa

[27] Finance. (n.d.). Retrieved June 20, 2017, from https://www.dataminr.com/finance

2.6 Existing Use Cases of Blockchain in Financial Industry

Like AI, applications for Blockchain technologies span across various industries. The major

use of Blockchain Technology in the financial sector is to develop cryptocurrencies such as

Bitcoin (the original Blockchain). Since Bitcoin, various other blockchains and crypto-

currencies have been developed[28]. Some of the major projects which utilise these crypto-

currencies are:

1) R3 Corda – is a distributed ledger platform designed to record, manage and
   synchronise financial agreements between regulated financial institutions[29]. It would
   eliminate much of the manual, time consuming effort currently required to keep
   disparate ledgers synchronised with each other. It would also allow for greater levels
   of code sharing than presently used in the financial industry, reducing the cost of
   financial services for everyone.

2) Ripple RTGS (Real-Time Gross Settlement) system – is a distributed cross-border
   payment network which does Real-time gross settlement. Multiple banks work with
   Ripple as clients to launch their own wallets[30]. On September 24, 2015 Rabobank
   started experimenting with Ethereum using Ripple's technology for it's smart cash
   wallet[31].

---

[28] CryptoCurrency Market Capitalizations. (n.d.). Retrieved June 20, 2017, from
https://coinmarketcap.com/all/views/all/

[29] Brown, R. G. (2016, April 05). Introducing R3 Corda™: A Distributed Ledger Designed for
Financial Services. Retrieved June 20, 2017, from
http://www.r3cev.com/blog/2016/4/4/introducing-r3-corda-a-distributed-ledger-designed-for-
financial-services

[30] Financial Institutions. (n.d.). Retrieved June 20, 2017, from
https://ripple.com/network/financial-institutions/

[31] Allison, I. (2015, September 24). Rabobank experiments with Ethereum via smart cash wallet.
Retrieved June 20, 2017, from http://www.ibtimes.co.uk/rabobank-experiments-ethereum-via-
smart-cash-wallet-1519910

3) Z cash – created by Zerocoin Electric Coin Company, Z cash is one of the safest crypto-currencies as it doesn't disclose the identity of the sender, the receiver or the details of the transaction[32]. The company uses ground-breaking cryptographic techniques to achieve this feat and strongly believe in the necessity of privacy in business and personal domains.

Because Blockchain is a nascent technology most of its other applications are still in POC phase or in initial stages. A few of these are:

1) NASDAQ Linq Platform – on December 30, 2015 NASDAQ (National Association of Securities Dealers Automated Quotations) announced that an issuer Chain.com used its Linq Blockchain Technology to successfully complete and record a private securities transaction[33]. This transaction was the first of its kind using the Blockchain Technology. It provides the issuer with a digital record of ownership and reduces the settlement time and need for a paper stock certificate. This same concept can be now extended to public markets.

2) CUBER, LHV Pank Estonia – CUBER stands for Cryptographic Universal Blockchain Entered Receivables. It is a new kind of Certificate of Deposit which issues receivables in the form of coloured coins. On May 14, 2015 LHV Pank (Lõhmus, Haavel & Viisemann) became the first bank to use this technology to issue €100,000 worth of cryptographically protected claims against the bank in Bitcoin blockchain[34].

---

[32] About Us. (n.d.). Retrieved June 20, 2017, from https://z.cash/about.html

[33] Nasdaq Linq Enables First-Ever Private Securities Issuance Documented With Blockchain Technology. (2015, December 30). Retrieved June 21, 2017, from http://ir.nasdaq.com/releasedetail.cfm?releaseid=948326

[34] CUBER – LHV Bank started public use of blockchain technology by issuing securities. (2015, June 08). Retrieved June 21, 2017, from http://www.cuber.ee/en_US/news/

Cuber Technology company, along with another Tech firm ChromeWay, has developed Cuber wallet application for fast and free P2P mobile flat currency payment. CUBER enables developers to build new financial services in traditional currencies. It is built on top of open coloured coin which uses Bitcoin Blockchain. Since LHV operates internationally they have followed in place regulations and thus this technology has helped provide a legal framework for Blockchain implementation in many countries.

3) Digital Asset – uses distributed technology to improve the efficiency, security, compliance and settlement speeds of asset management. The firm is backed by major banks such BNP Paribas, Citi, JP Morgan, Goldman Sachs etc[35]. On February 27, 2017 DTCC (Depository Trust and Clearing Corporation) announced successful completion of a POC to better manage netting process for US Treasury and Agency, Repurchase Agreement (Repo) transactions leveraging DTL, with Digital Asset. The project will now move to phase two which will align the technology with the needs on the $3 trillion per day Repo and related transactions in the industry[36].

4) BTL and Visa Cross-border Payment settlement project – BTL (Blockchain Technology Limited) with Visa explores ways in which Blockchain based settlements can reduce friction in the domestic and cross-border transfers between banks[37]. It will reduce costs, settlement time, credit risk and leverage smart contracts[38] to automate regulation and compliance requirements of domestic and international transfers.

---

[35] Digital Asset. (n.d.). Retrieved June 21, 2017, from https://www.digitalasset.com/index.html

[36] DTCC & Digital Asset Move to Next Phase After Successful Proof-Of-Concept for Repo Transactions Using Distributed Ledger Technology. (2017, February 27). Retrieved June 21, 2017, from http://www.dtcc.com/news/2017/february/27/dtcc-and-digital-asset-move-to-next-phase

[37] BTL & Visa. (n.d.). Retrieved June 21, 2017, from http://btl.co/visa/

[38] Investopedia. (2017, April 18). Smart Contracts. Retrieved June 21, 2017, from http://www.investopedia.com/terms/s/smart-contracts.asp

5) Utility Settlement Coins - a group of major banks; UBS, Deutsche Bank, Santander and BNY Mellon, as well as the broker NEX Group (formerly ICAP), has teamed up to develop a new form of digital cash that will help to set an industry standard to clear and settle financial trades over a distributed ledger[39]. It would be used for post-trade settlements between financial institutions on private financial platforms built on blockchain technology and permit settlement of trades in seconds rather than days with reduced risk and operational costs.

6) Hyperlegder Project[40] – it is an open source collaborative effort created to advance cross-industry blockchain technologies and is supported by many firms. It is a global collaboration platform, hosted by the Linux Foundation, including leaders in finance, banking, IoT, supply chain, manufacturing and technology[41]. It keeps track of major POCs in the fields of finance and healthcare industry and provides an overview of the latest developments in the Blockchain Technology.

2.7 Challenges / Risks with AI and Blockchain implementations

A panel of experts in the fields of AI and Blockchain discussed the applications and challenges involved with these technologies in the FinTech Forum organized by FTC (ibid., para 1.8). The challenges and risks discussed by these distinguished panellists cover all aspects published in other literatures as well.

---

[39] Prisco, G. (2016, August 25). Utility Settlement Coin Aims to Set Industry Standard for Central Banking Digital Cash. Retrieved June 21, 2017, from http://www.nasdaq.com/article/major-banks-developing-utility-settlement-coin-an-industry-standard-for-digital-central-bank-cash-cm670203

[40] Hyperledger Home. (n.d.). Retrieved June 21, 2017, from https://www.hyperledger.org/

[41] Hyperledger and IBM Blockchain. (n.d.). Retrieved June 21, 2017, from https://www.ibm.com/blockchain/hyperledger.html

Diedre Mulligan (Associate Professor, UC Berkeley School of Information) discussed the challenges in implementing AI in her presentation for the FTC convention (ibid., para 1.8) in the values at risk section. Here is a summary of the major challenges:

1) Privacy of Data – a lot of personal information is collected via social media and other sources and fed to an AI system in the form of unstructured Big Data. The privacy and security of this data is especially a concern in regions where collection of personal data is strictly regulated such as the European Union[42]. But restricting the input of data (i.e. data minimalization) could result in providing incorrect and insufficient data to the AI system which could result in a faulty output. It is necessary to carefully handle such regulations.

2) Autonomy of Machine – this factor determines how much control a machine has. Can it decide on its own or is human intervention necessary? Humans usually trust machines more than they trust other humans, but one needs to be careful as it is easy to lie with data. For this reason, a legal and ethical framework is needed. Also, certain regions in the world are more accepting of fully automatic machines while others, like Europe, are more sceptical and have stricter regulations. In 2016, the European Parliament's Legal Affairs Committee commissioned a study to evaluate and analyse, from a legal and ethical perspective, the future European civil laws and rules in robotics[43]. European Parliament has always been and is still concerned about autonomous nature of AI.

---

[42] Protection of personal data. (n.d.). Retrieved June 22, 2017, from
http://ec.europa.eu/justice/data-protection/

[43] Civil Law Rules on Robotic. (2017, March 01). Retrieved June 22, 2017, from
http://www.europarl.europa.eu/legislative-train/theme-area-of-justice-and-fundamental-rights/file-civil-law-rules-on-robotics

3) Fairness of Output – this is one of the most important challenge faced by an AI system. In the same presentation mentioned before by Professor Mulligan (ibid., para 1.8), explains types of bias and the ways in which they can be introduced in a system. Bias can be intentional (created by designer intentionally), due to faulty design (unintended design faults) or systemic (due to inaccurate training data in system). Designers need to be careful while profiling data to reduce bias as much as possible. If the data in the existing system is biased it needs to be properly filtered so that it does not propagate it into the digital system. If it is not possible to eliminate the bias completely, regulations must be in place to decide how much bias is acceptable and ensure that it doesn't lead to outright discrimination. In certain cases, bias might be intentional but it will need to be within the legal and ethical framework of the system.

4) Responsibility – it is necessary to address this concern specially to handle conflict resolutions arising from errors caused by an AI system. We need to carefully determine the responsible authority in case of a system failure. If AI system provides an incorrect output which leads to negative real-world consequences, regulations need to be in place to determine the accountability. The fault could arise from incorrect data, incorrect design or any other means and an audit system needs to be in place to verify it. There needs to be a system to ensure that adequate compensation and correction is provided in case of an error.

2.7.2 Challenges / Risks in Blockchain

For Blockchain technology the challenges and risks involved are well summarized by an article on Deloitte's forum[44]. This article addressed most of the issues discussed in

---

[44] Boersma, J., & Bulters, J. (2017, April 05). Blockchain technology: 9 benefits & 7 challenges | Deloitte. Retrieved June 22, 2017, from https://www2.deloitte.com/nl/nl/pages/innovatie/artikelen/blockchain-technology-9-benefits-and-7-challenges.html

the FTC convention (ibid., para 1.8). The major challenges facing Blockchain are:

1) Nascent Technology – resolving challenges such as the transaction speed, the verification process, and the data limits will be crucial in making blockchain widely applicable. The research in the field is still in initial stages as most firms are looking to adapt and customize the technology to their needs.

2) Uncertainty about regulations – because modern currencies have always been created and regulated by national governments, widespread adoption of cryptocurrencies by financial institutions will be difficult if the government regulation status remains same. Also, since the technology is still nascent it is not possible to efficiently regulate it as we never know how it would shape-up in the future. Specifically, permissioned blockchains (blockchains with restricted permission access) are impossible to fully regulate in their current form, and an industry standard needs to be developed for the same.

3) Large energy consumption – the Bitcoin blockchain miners are attempting 450 thousand trillion (4.5×10^{14}) solutions per second in efforts to validate transactions, and are using substantial amounts of computer power and electricity. There is a need to develop consensus mechanisms which will be economically and environmentally more efficient.

4) Security and Privacy concerns – even though solutions exist, cyber security concerns need to be addressed before people will entrust their personal data to a blockchain solution. Also, like AI privacy of the data is a major concern which can be somewhat mitigated using a private permissioned blockchains with strong encryption.

5) Transition to new system – switching to Blockchain applications would involve significant changes to, or a complete replacement of, existing systems. It is

necessary to have a smooth transition, for which the companies must strategize, while keeping in mind the regulatory and legal factors involved.

6) Cultural and behavioural acceptance – Blockchain represents a complete shift to a decentralized network which would require users and operators to make a cultural and behavioural shift. Most financial institutions today operate in a centralized system where an organisation establishes a trust-factor with its clients and builds a reputation. Relinquishing this control to a decentralized system and accepting a P2P consensus could produce challenges in conflict resolutions if proper regulations are not in place.

7) High instalment costs – even though Blockchain offers tremendous savings in transaction costs and time, the initial capital costs are high. It would be necessary for firms to thoroughly test POCs and analyse their financial structure and the gains before investing in the technology.

2.8 Integrating AI and Blockchain technologies

Considering the popularity of AI and Blockchain and the advantages they provide, some firms are investing in research to integrate the two to obtain more effective solutions. Even though the Blockchain technology is new, companies like AI Blockchain are already working towards integrating it with AI[45]. AI Blockchain technology is a user-friendly, transparent, energy efficient, digital ledger that maximizes security while remaining immutable and by employing artificial intelligent agents that govern the chain. Another financial asset management company, State Street (ibid., para 1.9), is working on a solution that would

---

[45] Blockchain Financial Services. (n.d.). Retrieved June 22, 2017, from http://ai-blockchain.com/blockchain-financial-services/

check investment data using AI and verify it using a cryptographically proven immutable

blockchain. Many other firms are also investing in such research including big tech firms

such as IBM[46].Trent McConaghy (Founder and CTO BigchainDB), published a paper in

December last year explaining the benefits of integrating these technologies[47]. Here is a

summary:

1) Data Sharing → Better Models – in contrast with traditional data storage methods

   which isolates data into silos, Blockchain allows sharing data and thus is perfect for

   AI system which need enormous amounts of data. This could happen in 3 ways:

   a) Within an organization

   b) Within an industry

   c) Globally or within public systems

   By sharing data, AI can identify if the cause of problems within one part of a system

   is related to a different part in the system. It could help in providing better auditing of

   the system and thus in cost savings.

2) Data Sharing → Qualitatively New Models – apart from improving existing models,

   sharing data could result in providing insights that could lead to building new models.

   This would allow us to do things which seemed to be impossible before. The effects

   again could be seen in all kinds of systems as stated before, i.e. within an

   organization, an industry or globally.

3) Audit trails on data and models for more trustworthy predictions – for an AI system

   "garbage-in, garbage-out" is an issue. If the input training data is faulty the output

---

[46] Del Castillo, M. (2016, June 10). IBM's New Watson Centre Merges Blockchain With AI.
Retrieved June 23, 2017, from http://www.coindesk.com/ibms-asia-watson-blockchain-ai/

[47] McConaghy, T. (2017, January 03). Blockchains for Artificial Intelligence – The
BigchainDB Blog. Retrieved June 23, 2017, from https://blog.bigchaindb.com/blockchains-
for-artificial-intelligence-ec63b0284984

will be faulty. Blockchain can help audit the input provided to AI systems by providing timestamps at each stage. This will help identify leaks in the data supply chain, and if an error is found, it can help track how and where it occurred.

4) Shared global registry of training data and models – what happens in one part of the globe could affect the other. AI needs valid datasets and Blockchains can be improved by better AI models. A global repository which allows people to share datasets and models would help improve both the technologies. Such a decentralized exchange will see the emergence of a truly open data market.

5) Data and models as IP assets → data and model exchange – data and models can be brought, sold or licensed as IP assets. Blockchain would provide tamper-resistant global public registry to store the claim to the copyright of the IP asset. It would also provide a tamper-resistant platform for licensing transactions and transfer of ownership with appropriate permissions.

6) AI DAO (Decentralized Autonomous Organizations) – are AI that can accumulate wealth, and that one can't turn off as it stores the state of the machine. It is the next level of smart contracts (autonomous code which runs a set of rules on Blockchain), it is a code that can own assets. To build an AI DAO start with an AI, and make it decentralized. Alternatively, begin the program with a DAO and grant it AI decision-making abilities.

2.9 Summary and Conclusion

This chapter briefly describes how AI and Blockchain technologies work. It provided a perspective on why Financial Institutions are investing in them and how they can be disruptive. It addressed the current applications of these technologies and how they are shaping the industry. It was also necessary to look at the challenges and risks involved in implementing these technologies. Lastly, there has been some research and work about integrating the features of AI and Blockchain to look for better solutions and the literature for this has also been put forward.

The purpose of this chapter was to provide an overview of the technologies and their applications in the financial sector. It listed out the findings which will be analysed for answers to the research questions posed in the first chapter. The next chapter, will address in detail at how the data was collected and its relevance.

CHAPTER 3 – RESEARCH METHODOLOGIES

3.1 Introduction

The purpose of this chapter is to describe in detail the research methodology followed in this dissertation. To conduct research, it is necessary to identify and define a research philosophy and a research methodology that are in sync with the objectives of the dissertation. What follows is a discussion about the various categories of research philosophies and methodologies and a justification of the best fit for this research. This chapter will describe in detail how the data was collected and analysed. We will also look at the methods followed to ensure that the data collected is reliable, valid and ethical.

3.2 Research Philosophy

A research philosophy helps to understand the beliefs and assumptions of the researcher. It provides an overview of what the researcher identifies as reality and truth and the researcher's perception of the facts. There are three types of philosophical paradigms; positivism, realism and interpretivism[48]. The first two are considered conventional methods whose central focus is on objectivism. In contrast interpretivism, or constructivism, denies the possibility of objective knowledge of the world. A research journal compares the two categories (Guba and Lincoln, 1989)[49]. Conventional methods consider theoretical facts and observations as independent entities, and thus are not effective for this research[50].

---

[48] Flowers, P. (January 2009). Research Philosophies – Importance and Relevance. Leading Learning and Change, (01), 1-5. Retrieved June 23, 2017, from http://blogs.warwick.ac.uk/files/cesphd/flowers_2009.pdf

[49] Guba, E. G.; Lincoln, Y. S. (1989). Fourth generation evaluation. London: Sage Publications.

[50] Stern, E. (2004). Philosophies and types of evaluation research. The foundations of evaluation and impact research, 1-44. Retrieved June 23, 2017, from www.cedefop.europa.eu/files/BgR1_Stern.pdf.

Constructivism on the other hand implies that facts and observations are interrelated and that relevant interpretation and evaluations can be carried out based on published literature. This dissertation, requires an analysis of facts presented in existing literature and evaluation of the same, for which constructivism is more appropriate philosophy to adopt.

3.3 Research Methodology

Research methodologies describes the framework followed to conduct a research study. There are primarily eight types of research methodologies[51] and they can be classified into four categories which contrast with each other:

- descriptive vs analytical – are the facts only described (descriptive) or are they being analysed and evaluated (analytical) to look for a solution?
- applied vs fundamental – will the solution obtained from the research be applied to a problem (action based – applied) or is a theory being formulated (fundamental)?
- quantitative vs qualitative – what kind of data is being analysed numerical (quantitative) or behavioural (qualitative)?
- conceptual vs empirical – what is the research based upon, formulated concepts and theories (conceptual) or observations (empirical)?

These methodologies can be used individually or in combination depending on the aims and objectives of the research. As the aim of this dissertation is to put forward facts and analyse them, an analytical research methodology is most appropriate.

---

[51] Kothari, C.R. (n.d.). Research Methodology Methods & Techniques (2nd ed.). New Delhi: New Age International.

3.4 Data Collection

The data collected and put forward in this dissertation is secondary data collected from reliable sources in the form of articles, journals and other literature on the subject[52]. Relevant and up-to-date data on the subject is easily available from multiple sources and hence the research is purely theoretical. To understand the blockchain, the original whitepaper on Bitcoin can be referred which explains in detail the features of the Bitcoin blockchain. Literature on AI was obtained from multiple research papers published by reputed universities on the subject which explain the technology and its history.

Due to a recent surge in research on both AI and Blockchain, up-to-date information on the technologies is available on the internet (as recent as June 2017). Open source forums like Hyperledger keep track of the latest POCs in Blockchain. There are multiple conferences on AI which provide the latest developments in the technology. In addition, various financial institutions and tech companies have published white papers on the applications of AI and Blockchain in the financial industry which provide details about the use cases already implemented and the ones in pipeline for the future. Information on the subject is also available on various online forums and blogs by experts in the field. The important task was thus to filter and validate the available information.

3.5 Reliability, Validity and Ethics

Since the data collected for this dissertation was purely theoretical it was necessary to ensure that the source of the data was valid and reliable. Data was abundantly available so filtering

---

[52] Kumar, R. (2011). RESEARCH METHODOLOGY a step-by-step guide for beginners (3rd ed.). Los Angeles: Sage Publications.

was necessary to ensure that the material discussed in the papers or articles was relevant to the technologies and the financial industry and that it was in sync with the objectives of this dissertation[53].

The literature put forward in this dissertation was obtained from research materials published by field experts from reputed institutions (educational or commercial). The date of the publication was checked to verify the information is up-to-date and further research was conducted to check if any recent updates are available on the topic. The original sources from the published materials were also checked to ascertain the reliability of the articles.

To ascertain whether research is credible, it is necessary to be ethical. The principal behind ethical research is to cause no harm. It is necessary especially in the literature review section to provide source of information and provide valid citations for the original work to avoid plagiarism. At every stage in the research all ethical guidelines were followed.

---

[53] Walliman, N. (2011). *RESEARCH METHODS THE BASICS*. London: Routledge.

CHAPTER 4 – DISCUSSION AND ANALYSIS

4.1 Introduction

In the literature review chapter, we looked at the AI and Blockchain technologies, their benefits, challenges and applications. The purpose of this chapter is to discuss and analyse the data presented to answer the research questions put forward before. We will first look at the issues and challenges faced by the financial industry with respect to application of AI and Blockchain. We will also look at the possible applications of integrating these technologies and what the future holds for them in the financial industry.

4.2 Challenges of AI and Blockchain implementation in the Financial Industry?

Even though AI has progressed considerably in recent years its applications in the financial industry are not as widespread as we see in the Tech industry. Blockchain technology originated within the financial industry almost a decade ago (ibid., para 2.16) but it is still not widely adapted. This could be due to several factors and, in this section, and we will discuss a few of them here.

4.2.1 Need for higher security

Compared to any other industry the need for security and data protection is much higher in the financial industry. For a financial firm to succeed in the industry it needs to build trust with its clients and customers. Any breach in security could be disastrous for the firm. For example, if your bank account gets hacked it is much worse than if your Facebook account gets hacked. The real-world consequences of a security threat to a financial institution are severe. Therefore, financial institutions are overly conscious about implementing technologies which have security concerns.

Cyber-security is a real threat. AI models need massive amounts of data for processing and building accurate models. A lot of data in financial institutions is confidential and providing this data to an AI system without proper security could be harmful. A system which is perfectly safe when running standalone could be susceptible to attack when integrated with an unsafe environment such as the internet. Blockchain technology is also not entirely free from attacks, the Ethereum blockchain faced a Denial of Service (DoS) 51% attack last year[54]. The problem with a Blockchain system is that security lies with the end user. If you transfer a bitcoin to a wrong address only the receiver has the power to reverse the authority, unlike in the current banking system where a central controlling authority can reverse an incorrect transaction. Hence, if a blockchain network gets hacked and fake transactions are executed they can't be reversed because the system is immutable.

Another drawback of using the AI and Blockchain technologies is that it makes the data susceptible to surveillance (also by national governments, which can be problematic in certain countries). AI uses Big Data which can't be audited by humans and allows for possibilities of data leakage. Data on the Blockchain is distributed and is thus accessible to every node on the network. There are chances of the data falling into the wrong hands. This risk can be slightly mitigated by using permissioned blockchains which provide access only to certain authorised users but this technology needs to be perfected. Therefore, until better methods are devised to ensure security of data financial institutions will be sceptical about fully embracing these technologies. Also, they will need to ensure that all stakeholders are aware of the risks.

---

[54] Hertig, A. (2016, October 07). So, Ethereum's Blockchain is Still Under Attack... Retrieved June 25, 2017, from http://www.coindesk.com/so-ethereums-blockchain-is-still-under-attack/

4.2.2 Shortfalls of the Technologies

There are various shortcomings in both the technologies which makes their
implementation difficult in the financial sector. AI models can't be generic to all
firms. The same AI model running on different data set will produce different results.
For example, if a developer designs a generic AI model to identify potential clients
for insurance companies, depending on the data provided by each firm for similar
schemes the outputs could be very different. It depends on the data history and the
clarity of data set provided to the model. Also, AI models are usually designed to
handle generalization, we need to be very careful with the outliers and the exceptional
cases. For example, a person applying for a loan from a bank could be rejected by an
AI system for reasons which in real world would not be valid cause for rejection. This
could happen because the system finds data in the applicant's proposal which though
relevant does not fit the AI model. Gaps or blind-spots in the data could result in an
inaccurate model which could cost the firms potential clients.

AI systems are extremely susceptible to bias. As discussed in the literature review,
bias can be of multiple types. Intentional bias could be dangerous, as a designer might
have a malicious intent and could keep secret loopholes in the system which could
later be utilised for personal gains. This could lead to fraud and be costly to the firms.
If bias is introduced by faulty design or incorrect data it could result in problems like
the ones discussed earlier. As stated by Professor Rayid Ghani in the FTC conference
(ibid., para 1.8), in an AI model there could be a trade-off between privacy, accuracy
and bias. The best model will depend on the priorities set by the designer. If the model
needs to be private and accurate, we might have to accept some amount of bias (but it
needs to be within the legal framework).

The original Bitcoin Blockchain (ibid., para 1.9) is unsuitable for financial institutions particularly due to its low scalability. The consensus mechanism for Bitcoin Blockchain takes 10 minutes to validate a block of transactions. Banks are usually dealing with thousands of transactions per second. Since Bitcoin, various other faster blockchains were developed but scalability is still not as high as expected. The reason for this is, even though the Blockchain technology runs on multiple nodes the processing power is not augmented by addition of each node. In fact, the processing will advance at the rate of the slowest node in the system. Much of the research in Blockchain is hence directed towards increasing the scalability of the technology

4.2.3 Issues with Regulations and Standardization

AI has evolved considerably in the recent years and Blockchain is still a nascent technology, and hence both these technologies do not have strong and effective regulations. This is a concern for financial institutions who face huge regulatory fines for non-compliance and spend a lot on compliance related activities. Because the technologies are evolving, regulators are unable to predict how they would shape up in the future and thus predict the loopholes to regulate effectively. There is also the fear that over-regulating could stifle innovation in the sector.

Lack of regulation creates concerns because firms have no clarity on what course to follow in a case of conflicting scenarios. For example, if one of the European nodes on a Blockchain network receives a transaction from troubled regions like Syria, it would raise a flag. But how should the network respond and who should take the responsibility to audit the transaction in a decentralized system? The regulations today are designed to provide guidelines and best practices for a centrally controlled financial institution. They provide an ethical framework based on where the control lies. The regulatory framework will need to evolve to accommodate a decentralized technology such as Blockchain. In case of a fraud, there is currently no system to fall back on and no system for conflict resolution.

AI technology is better regulated than Blockchain but it can still have plenty of loopholes which are unknown to regulators yet and which could be exploited. In the literature review chapter, we have discussed how different regions in the world react to data protection (ibid., para 2.25) and autonomous machines (ibid., para 3.25). We have also talked in the previous case about how same AI model can produce different results based on different data sets. Standardization is necessary to ensure unbiased results and better models. The same is true in the case of Blockchains. If every firm develops a customized Blockchain, integration will be difficult and it will result in a chaotic system. A standardized system will also be much easier to regulate.

4.2.4 Other Challenges

We have already seen that implementation of Blockchain technology would require a complete restructure or major changes to the existing financial system. A central body which has the authority and control over its actions will be replaced by a completely decentralized P2P network of equally powerful nodes. This would result in transfer of power to establish trust from a single controlled organization to a decentralized network of nodes. The reason why financial institutions might be unwilling to immediately accept this decentralized network is because they are not aware of the effects it would have on the firm, after the control is relinquished.

In general, Financial firms are usually slower than Tech firms to adapt to innovation. But in this case, it would be behavioural change not only for the firms, but also for the clients of these firms as well. People are used to banks handling their finances. They know who is in control and who is responsible in case of issues. There exists a system of insurance in case of frauds. A decentralized system, will be a complete shift to a new structure. It is necessary to have a legal and stable framework to fall back on for conflict resolution to protect the rights of clients in case of issues. At this stage, if financial firms move ahead with the implementation of this technology and it faces security threats, it could result in discrediting the firm as well as harm the innovation in the technology itself. People might be sceptical to accept it in the future.

For an AI system, it is necessary to ensure that it performs its tasks at least as well as if not better than its human counterpart. If the AI model is faulty it could result in real-world consequences for the firm and its clients. AI systems work by finding correlations in Big Data and thus it is necessary that the system understands that correlation is not causation. European laws which promote data minimalization (ibid., para 2.25) were addressed in the literature review chapter. This restriction of data to AI can produce a faulty AI model as it will not have sufficient data to make a properly informed decision. For example, AI model is not designed correctly a chat bot which provides investment advice, could make wrong investment decision for the client.

4.3 Possible use cases of integrating features of AI and Blockchain technologies

In the literature review chapter, we talked about a few firms which are working on integrating the features of AI and Blockchains and the possible benefits of doing the same. After analysing the various use cases presented before there could be several ways in which firms could work together to produce better results with these technologies.

1) Integration of Veridas with Blockchain – as discussed Veridas (ibid., para 2.19), is a firm that uses AI for biometric data verification of clients. Also, financial institutions invest a lot on KYC related activities (ibid., para 3.17) and there is a need for a shared KYC registry. This need for a shared registry is demonstrated by the success of

SWIFT KYC registry[55]. SWIFT member banks share KYC details, but they do not use AI technologies. A possible use case would be to use the biometric analysis AI capabilities of Veridas and embed them on a distributed Blockchain which is then shared between financial institutions. This would remove duplication of efforts and result in cost savings. Also, since the data would be on a blockchain and shared between all nodes, the chances of a single institution taking control or an attack would be mitigated.

2) Everledger for Financial Assets – Everledger is a firm that validates and provides certifications (proof-of-ownership) to high net worth assets such as diamonds using Blockchain[56]. Similar concepts can be introduced for financial assets. AI model can be designed to analyse the value of the asset to check for frauds and other security threats and a Blockchain could then be used to certify the asset. This would create a cryptographic digital proof of ownership for the asset. This is a similar concept to the asset IP benefit of combining AI and Blockchain mentioned previously.

3) Smart Contracts – these are self-executing digital contracts embedded on a Blockchain. Chamber of Digital Commerce has initiated a Smart Contract Alliance to promote the use of smart contracts[57]. So far, these contracts use code with if-else loops[58] to execute the contract terms. Another use case of this technology could be to

---

[55] SWIFT's KYC Registry crosses 3,000-member milestone. (2016, November 22). Retrieved June 25, 2017, from https://www.swift.com/news-events/press-releases/swift_s-kyc-registry-crosses-3_000-member-milestone

[56] Volpicelli, G. (2017, February 15). How the blockchain is helping stop the spread of conflict diamonds. Retrieved June 25, 2017, from http://www.wired.co.uk/article/blockchain-conflict-diamonds-everledger

[57] Smart Contracts Alliance. (n.d.). Retrieved June 25, 2017, from https://digitalchamber.org/initiatives/smart-contracts-alliance/

[58] JavaScript If...Else Statements. (n.d.). Retrieved June 25, 2017, from https://www.w3schools.com/js/js_if_else.asp

enhance the features of these contracts using an AI model instead of a normal code. AI would be better suited to identify frauds and loopholes in the execution than any other program. It would help make these contracts smarter and secure.

The possibilities in this domain could be tremendous. Both the technologies are evolving and new user cases and POCs are carried out every month. As the features develop, new and unforeseen possibilities could emerge. Further research can be carried out to identify better use cases and implementations of these integrated systems.

4.4 The future of AI and Blockchain in Financial Industry

This paper has listed the features and benefits that AI and Blockchain have provided so far and it is now time to look at the future. Some of the projects mentioned before are already planning for its next phase. For example, the Digital Asset's Repo transaction system (ibid., para 2.23), discussed earlier, is planning to launch Phase 2 in early 2018 which is targeting global Repo transactions. Some of the other possibilities for these technologies in the future could be:

1) Crypto-currencies – banks and governments switch from paper currency and electronic cash to completely digital and secure cryptocurrencies as general purpose official money. It is only a matter of time until the system becomes stable and secure from attacks. If paper currencies get replaced by crypto-currencies it would provide environmental benefits as well.

2) Social-media credit scoring – firms like Big Data Scoring are making headway in using Big Data for credit scoring for people who lack appropriate credit history, such as millennials. The technology is still emerging and the firm has partnered

with Master Card[59]. The same model can be used to improve other types of credit scoring techniques.

3) Public Securities Trading – the private securities transaction carried out by Chain.com using NASDAQ's Linq platform (ibid., para 3.22) could be used as a POC and extended to public markets. All Public securities transactions would then be done via a secure decentralized blockchain providing faster settlement times and thus cost benefits.

4) Advisor Bots – chat bots are a common phenomenon these days, especially for customer support, but they are not as prevalent with financial institutions. With appropriate AI models, such as the ones used in Binatix (ibid., para 1.20), they can be used as financial advisors. These bots could be developed with NLC such that they would respond to clients just as a human advisor would.

5) Financial Inclusion – in the FTC conference (ibid., para 1.8) Perianne Boring (President of Chamber of Digital Commerce) brought up this issue. She pointed out that billions of people do not have access to basic banking facilities, but many of these people do have access to smart phones. Disruptive technologies like AI and Blockchain could hence be used to reach out to these people and provide them with secure banking capabilities via smart phone capabilities.

6) Removal of Intermediaries – one of the major impact of shifting to Blockchain would be the removal of third party intermediaries in trading. These intermediaries charge huge fees to perform credibility checks to ensure trust between trading parties as the trust-factor. A decentralized blockchain would make these intermediaries worthless and provide cost benefits to firms and clients.

---

[59] THE LEADER IN BIG DATA CREDIT SCORING SOLUTIONS. (n.d.). Retrieved June 25, 2017, from http://bigdatascoring.com/

7) Protected blockchains – as we've discussed before the major roadblock to implementation of AI and Blockchain technologies is security. But there are also extremely secure Blockchains such as Z cash (ibid., para 1.22). If the cryptographic benefits of Z cash are perfected, customized, scaled and adapted to other Blockchains and utilised in AI models it could provide the security features required for financial institutions to adapt technologies faster.

There could be various other possibilities and use cases. New benefits and applications will come forward as the technologies evolve and as people adapt to these changes.

CHAPTER 5 – CONCLUSION

5.1 Introduction

This dissertation, has discussed the literature on AI and Blockchain technologies. It has also looked at the research methodologies used to collect the data. The literature was analysed to identify the various challenges faced in the financial industry and to look for opportunities in the future for these technologies. The purpose of this chapter is to summarize all the data and explain how these technologies have proved to be disruptive to the financial industry.

5.2 How disruptive are AI and Blockchain technologies?

AI and Blockchain are here to stay. There are risks and challenges in the implementations but the net potential benefits outweigh these drawbacks. Even though the Financial Industry has been slow in adopting these technologies the scenario is steadily improving.

A lot of POCs have already been carried out. Most banks and financial institutions are partnering with AI and Blockchain firms or have set up their own research labs. Many white papers and research papers have been published on these technologies and their applications. Multiple conferences are being held to identify possible use cases and discuss challenges. Experts in the field are working with regulators to provide guidelines and to set up best practices to promote the growth and innovation in the field. The regulators are also trying to ensure that consumer rights are protected in the process.

Technologies evolve with time and people evolve with them, and learn to adapt to them, as was the case with internet in the late nineties. It took decades for the technology behind internet to come to the stage that it is at now. The same is true for AI. AI has been a part of science fiction for decades but it slowly developed to the technology that Facebook now uses to tag our photos or Amazon uses to recommend us products to buy. Tech companies have been a major factor to develop AI capabilities. A similar trend could develop with DLT and Blockchain, especially with the advent of FinTech industry which encompasses the benefits of both Financial and Tech industries.

It is too early to predict how these technologies will overcome their challenges and evolve individually or together. There is also the possibility that an alternative technology is discovered which might replace these two and provide better solutions. It will be very interesting to see how they shape up, but looking at the pace at which they are evolving it is likely that they might turn out to be a necessity in the future, just like internet turned out to be what it is today.

5.3 Research Limitations

The primary limitation of this research is that the data collected is only secondary data from published sources. Even though the data is sufficient to understand the technologies and their applications, further insights could be obtained by using primary data collection techniques such as field observations and interviews.

A visit to an AI or Blockchain firm would provide better understanding of the applications of these technologies in the sector, the impact it has in the real-world and the economic benefits the technologies provides to the firm and its clients. Also, interviews with experts in the field or with employees of an AI or Blockchain firm would provide better understanding of the technologies. It would also provide a first-hand view of the challenges the firm or its employees face while working with these technologies.

Another limitation of this research would be the perspective of the researcher towards the technologies. The focus was entirely on identifying the use cases and applications of the technologies and looking towards the benefits. A thorough analysis of the drawbacks also needs to be carried out before moving ahead with the applications.

5.4 Areas for Further Research

Since the application of both the technologies is still not widespread in the financial industry there is a lot of scope for further research, specifically in the integration of AI and Blockchain. The applications of the technologies can be looked in more details and POCs can be conducted to address the challenges faced. The analytical research method can be supplemented by other research methodologies such as field studies (qualitative research) to obtain further understanding of the technologies and their applications. A research can also be conducted to identify the drawbacks and risks and alternative technologies which could provide better solutions to the industry.

BIBLIOGRAPHY

- Artificial Intelligence Won't Solve The Financial Services Industry's Problems. (2016, June 08). Retrieved May 10, 2017, from https://www.cbinsights.com/blog/artificial-intelligence-and-fintech-competition/

- Artificial intelligence in financial services. (n.d.). Retrieved June 09, 2017, from https://www.pwc.com/us/en/financial-services/research-institute/artificial-intelligence.html

- Backed by LHV Bank and ChromaWay. (n.d.). Retrieved May 15, 2017, from http://www.cuber.ee/

- BANKING ON BLOCKCHAIN (White paper). (2016, January). Retrieved May 22, 2017, from Finextra IBM website: https://www.ingwb.com/media/1609652/banking-on-blockchain.pdf

- Banking on the Future: Vision 2020 (Working paper). (2016, September). Retrieved May 12, 2017, from CII-Deloitte website: https://www2.deloitte.com/content/dam/Deloitte/in/Documents/financial-services/in-fs-deloitte-banking-colloquium-thoughtpaper-cii.pdf

- Ben-Ari, A. (2017, January 25). Outstanding Challenges in Blockchain Technology in 2017. Retrieved June 13, 2017, from https://appliedblockchain.com/outstanding-challenges-in-blockchain-2017/

- Bendor-Samuel, P. (2017, May 23). The Primary Challenge To Blockchain Technology. Retrieved June 12, 2017, from https://www.forbes.com/sites/peterbendorsamuel/2017/05/23/the-primary-challenge-to-blockchain-technology/2/#4f7b8c717a12

- Biondi, D., Hetterscheidt, T., & Obermeier, B. (2016). Blockchain in the financial services industry (White paper). Retrieved May 24, 2017, from HP Enterprise website: https://www.hpe.com/h20195/v2/GetPDF.aspx/4AA6-5864ENW.pdf

- Blockchain in Banking: A Measured Approach (White paper). (2016, April). Retrieved May 24, 2017, from Cognizant website: https://www.cognizant.com/whitepapers/Blockchain-in-Banking-A-Measured-Approach-codex1809.pd

- Blockchain Services for Banking and Financial Services (White paper). (2016). Retrieved May 21, 2017, from Capgemini website: https://www.capgemini.com/resource-file-access/resource/pdf/blockchain_services_2016.pdf

- Blockchain Startup Investment Bounces Back. (2017, April 28). Retrieved May 10, 2017, from https://www.cbinsights.com/blog/blockchain-bitcoin-startup-funding/

- Brown, R. G., Carlyle, J., Grigg, I., & Hearn, M. (2016, August). Corda: An Introduction (Tech.). Retrieved May 15, 2017, from https://docs.corda.net/_static/corda-technical-whitepaper.pdf

- Buterin, V. (n.d.). A NEXT GENERATION SMART CONTRACT & DECENTRALIZED APPLICATION PLATFORM (Tech.). Retrieved May 16, 2017, from Ethereum.org website: http://www.the-blockchain.com/docs/Ethereum_white_paper-a_next_generation_smart_contract_and_decentralized_application_platform-vitalik-buterin.pdf

- Everledger secures the first bottle of wine on the blockchain. (2016, December 09). Retrieved May 13, 2017, from https://www.finextra.com/pressarticle/67381/everledger-secures-the-first-bottle-of-wine-on-the-blockchain

- Four Blockchain Use Cases for Banks (White paper). (2016). Retrieved May 20, 2017, from FinTech Network website: http://blockchainapac.fintecnet.com/uploads/2/4/3/8/24384857/fintech_blockchain_report_v3.pdf

- Funding to Artificial Intelligence Startups Reaches New Quarterly High. (2016, July 17). Retrieved May 10, 2017, from https://www.cbinsights.com/blog/artificial-intelligence-funding-trends-q216/

- Greener, S. (2008). Business Research Methods. Ventus Publishing.

- Iansiti, M., & Lakhani, K. (2017, February 17). The Truth About Blockchain. Retrieved June 10, 2017, from https://hbr.org/2017/01/the-truth-about-blockchain

- Introducing the Digital Asset Modeling Language. (n.d.). Retrieved May 17, 2017, from https://www.digitalasset.com/press/introducing-daml.html

- Koning, P. (2016). Artificial Intelligence (AI) for Financial Services (Rep.). Retrieved May 23, 2017, from Simularity website: http://simularity.com/wp-content/uploads/2016/11/Simularity-White-Paper-Driving-AI-for-Financial-Services-11-4pk.pdf

- Lamberton, C., Hoy, D., & Brigo, D. (2017, May). Impact of Robotics, RPA and AI on the insurance industry: challenges and opportunities. Retrieved June 08, 2017, from https://fsinsights.ey.com/big-issues/Digital-and-connectivity/shaping-insurance-robotics-rpa-and-ai

- Laurent, P., Cholette, T., & Herzberg, E. (n.d.). Intelligent automation entering the business world (Working paper). Retrieved May 22, 2017, from Deloitte website: https://www2.deloitte.com/content/dam/Deloitte/lu/Documents/operations/lu-intelligent-automation-business-world.pdf

- Leading the pack in blockchain banking (Executive Report). (2016, September). Retrieved May 18, 2017, from IBM Corporation website: https://public.dhe.ibm.com/common/ssi/ecm/gb/en/gbp03467usen/GBP03467USEN.PDF

- MacDonald, S., & Headlam, N. (n.d.). Research Methods Handbook. Centre for Local Economic Strategies. Retrieved June 12, 2017, from http://www.cles.org.uk/wp-content/uploads/2011/01/Research-Methods-Handbook.pdf

- Mkansi, M., & Acheampong, E. A. (2012). Research Philosophy Debates and Classifications: Students' Dilemma. The Electronic Journal of Business Research Methods, 10(2), 1-9. Retrieved June 15, 2017, from http://www.ejbrm.com

- Nevejans, N. (2016, October). European Civil Law Rules in Robotics. Retrieved June 01, 2017, from http://www.europarl.europa.eu/RegData/etudes/STUD/2016/571379/IPOL_STU(2016)57137 9_EN.pdf

- Padmanabhan, G. R., & Sivaramakrishnan, A. (2016, June 29). Reimagining K Y C Using Blockchain Technology (White paper). Retrieved May 18, 2017, from Tata Consultancy Services website: http://234w.tc.tracom.net/SiteCollectionDocuments/White-Papers/Reimagining-KYC-Blockchain-0716-1.pdf

- The KYC Registry. (2017, March 21). Retrieved May 16, 2017, from https://www.swift.com/our-solutions/compliance-and-shared-services/financial-crime-compliance/the-kyc-registry#topic-tabs-menu

- The New Wave of Artificial Intelligence (White paper). (2016). Retrieved May 23, 2017, from EVRY website: https://www.evry.com/globalassets/insight/bank2020/the-new-wave-of-artificial-intelligence---labs-whitepaper.pdf

- The Race For AI: Google, Twitter, Intel, Apple In A Rush To Grab Artificial Intelligence Startups. (2017, March 30). Retrieved May 10, 2017, from https://www.cbinsights.com/blog/top-acquirers-ai-startups-ma-timeline/

- The Rise of AI in Financial Services (Research Brief). (2016, June). Retrieved May 19, 2017, from Narrative Science website: https://narrativescience.com/Offers/The-Rise-of-AI-in-Financial-Services

- Top financial services issues of 2017 (Issue brief). (2016, December). Retrieved May 14, 2017, from PWC website: https://www.pwc.com/us/en/financial-services/research-institute/assets/pwc-top-financial-services-issues-2017.pdf

- Van Bommel, E., & Blanchard, M. (2016). Tomorrow's AI-Enabled Banking (Working paper). Retrieved May 21, 2017, from IP Soft website: http://www.ipsoft.com/wp-content/themes/ipsoft_v2/images/v2/pdf/IPsoft_Tomorrow_AI_enabled_banking.pdf

- Volpicelli, G. (2016, June 08). Beyond bitcoin. Your life is destined for the blockchain. Retrieved May 12, 2017, from http://www.wired.co.uk/article/future-of-the-blockchain

- Welcome to the digital vault of the future. (n.d.). Retrieved May 15, 2017, from https://www.everledger.io/

- Williams, A. (2016, August 25). How Facebook can affect your credit score. Retrieved June 16, 2017, from https://www.ft.com/content/e8ccd7b8-6459-11e6-a08a-c7ac04ef00aa?mhq5j=e2

- Wood, G. (n.d.). ETHEREUM: A SECURE DECENTRALISED GENERALISED TRANSACTION LEDGER (Tech.). Retrieved May 15, 2017, from http://gavwood.com/paper.pdf